CREATING A LIFE WORTH LIVING

VOLUME 3
EXPANDING YOUR WORLD VIEW

DEBBIE N. GOLDBERG

BALBOA.
PRESS

A DIVISION OF HAY HOUSE

Balboa Press books may be ordered through booksellers or by contacting:

Balboa Press
A Division of Hay House
1663 Liberty Drive
Bloomington, IN 47403
www.balboapress.com
1 (877) 407-4847

Print information available on the last page.

ISBN: 978-1-5043-5897-2 (sc)
ISBN: 978-1-5043-5898-9 (e)

Library of Congress Control Number: 2016909226

Balboa Press rev. date: 09/26/2016

This volume is about the gift of
life and valuing others in order
to expand your worldview.

It is about undertaking a journey that
will take courage, complete honesty,
openness, patience, compassion, faith,
persistence, and a commitment to your
self to create a loving purposeful life.

These books are a gift of love from
Spirit. They are a guide to love,
peace, purpose and healing.

Creating A Life Worth Living is a series of books that build upon each other and should be read in sequence to get the most out of them.

It would be helpful to read one chapter and then take time to think about the message and try to integrate it into your understanding before moving on to the next chapter.

Dedications, Acknowledgements, Preface & Background

In Volume 1 I acknowledged all those who have been part of my spiritual journey and who have touched these books in preparation for their release. I also included background information about myself and the circumstances that prompted me to start down my spiritual path. Please refer back to Volume 1 if you are interested in this information.

These books are also dedicated to all of you, through Jesus. They are a channeled message from Jesus that needs to be heard in order for everyone to live a life worth living, a life of happiness, gratitude, love and purpose.

I pray blessings that these books bring you to a place of co-creation of your life's purpose. God – Please bestow the blessings you have bestowed onto me to the readers of these books; heal me and heal them.

Awakening from the sleep/ unconsciousness, healing and following the spiritual journey is the hardest, most rewarding and most fulfilling work I have ever done. Don't be afraid. The work you are about to do is a gift to your self and becomes much easier as you paddle down the river of life with guidance, love, passion and purpose.

My precious heart pounds with the glory of God's grace upon me. I had never experienced love and beauty until I allowed my heart to be filled with pure joy. Hark! Are you listening? You too have a heart that sings out "Follow me, follow me, I will not disappoint you. You are the most beautiful light. Your light needs to shine so others can find their own light. Be brave. Be bold. Unleash the fears and chains that tie you to a life not worth living. Seek me. Find me. For I am yours forever through eternity."

Jesus (Channeled through me)

My strength is within you. Find it.
I left it there for you to seek. Never
stop; you must take it. For you will
need it to come back home and connect
with me. Savor it. It is yours and only
yours. It holds all the blessings and
abundance for your soul. Grasp it;
never let it go. Others will try to take
it, condemn it. Hold on tight to it,
for jealousy and greed will try to rip
it from you. Never let go; it is yours.
Protect it, shield it, honor it; it is yours.
It is the only thing that is yours.

God (Channeled through me)

It is happiness you say you want. It is already within you. Why do you not accept it? Why do you fear it? There are no strings attached. It is your divine privilege. No one can take it from you but you. Why do you give away such a treasure that is meant for you? It is yours only.

Jesus (Channeled through me)

Artist's Biography

Jane Tomlinson has a Master of Art Education. She taught high school fine art for thirty-one years in the Central Bucks School District, Bucks County, Pennsylvania. Jane is retired and living in the Florida Keys. She has become a member of the Art Guild of the Purple Isles as well as the Florida Keys Council of the Arts. She is also a practicing professional photographer. Jane has worked for a local glass artist designing and creating fused dichroic glass jewelry and art pieces. She now spends her time in the Keys painting, photographing and learning about the plants that thrive in that tropical environment. She is inspired daily with the natural beauty of the Florida Keys.

About the Author

Debbie N. Goldberg has been a therapist for 18 years practicing in Pennsylvania. She specializes in mental health and substance abuse issues, providing services to adults and couples. She has worked in a variety of settings and is now in private practice, residing in Islamorada Florida. She brings the spiritual knowledge of her own awakening into her work with others to inspire healing, love, joy, purpose and creativity through their own spiritual journey.

This series of books are channeled from her own spiritual guidance and incorporates teachings from Dr. Margaret Paul's Inner Bonding Program and Dr. Barbara De Angelis' Ultimate Program.

Contents

Chapter One

The Gift of life

Most people do not see the happiness and peace that resides in them. It is a quite place within your heart that you come to know. It holds the beauty of who you are and welcomes the opportunity to be one with you.

We are given so many gifts that we just don't understand, or see and take for granted. We need to protect and honor each of these gifts, especially the gift of life.

We can take life for granted, not just our own life, but every living thing or non-living thing around us. Believe it or not, everything serves a purpose, everything. For the most part, that purpose is you. Everything in this world is designed to support you, love you, and awaken you from your story, your illusion. It is easy to complain about all that is wrong and not focus on what is right. Our perception is how we view our story, our illusion. If we have been carrying pain then we will see everything through a lens of pain, fear and negativity. If we have had more positive lives, then we will see life through a more positive lens, although we still have fears that affect our whole life.

Yes, our souls have been evolving through many incarnations and carry these energetic vibrational memories and lessons into each successive lifetime so that we can continue to learn what it is that we need to evolve. I've often wondered why it is that I've worked so hard and learned so much but still have 'body memories' or the energetic vibration of trauma, fear, and sadness. Why do I feel so unsafe? There is a journal entry with Jesus later on in this book where he shares that all of us carry a fierce energy of fear, darkness and feeling unsafe since the beginning of man.

I talked before about having set points. Since I have lived many lives being unsafe (so I am told, because I do not remember) and experienced deep sadness, that energy continues to linger (which is what I feel). That's why our healing process takes time. We all need to heal lifetimes of negative energy, not just the pain and sadness that we may be experiencing in our present life, but generations of family energy as well. It is similar to having a disease and needing to undergo a long period of treatment and rehabilitation in order to be completely healed energetically.

This release or discharge of the accumulated energy is subtle and lengthy. The more you are able to connect to God/Spirit as an everyday practice, willing to hear or listen and heal your wounds, the more quickly your lessons will be learned and the negative energy will leave you. Begin using deep breathing exercises to help dissipate this energy.

Your job is to not plug into that negative energy. In order to avoid doing this, you have to be aware of what is within. Observe your thoughts, feelings, and response patterns. Understand that you are dealing with old energy that no longer serves you, look at it, feel it and let it go. Breathe it out. Spend some time each day to meditate, bask in the light of divine love and be at peace. You'll rejuvenate your body, mind and soul.

We're all impatient. We all want immediate gratification. We all want release from our negative energy and pain. Our tendency is to desperately look for some quick fix outside of us to stop the negative energy or thoughts, to give us peace, or push the feelings down, but this is suppression, self-abandonment and denial.

We really don't understand the power we have to heal ourselves. We have all heard of miracles where someone was deathly ill and all of a sudden they were healed. Some things happen instantaneously and some take longer. The power of prayer is amazing. Please don't take this as a suggestion that you shouldn't go to a doctor if you are ill. That isn't what I am saying. I just want you to recognize the power you have within for yourself and for blessing others.

We have all of God's/Spirit's Kingdom within us. It is there for us to access all the time. This is another gift of life that is not in our awareness for most of us. Your spiritual guidance has been working with you throughout your life even though you may not have been aware of it. We need to help ourselves by connecting to it tapping-in to it, and we do this through being quiet, meditating, praying, or creating. The more we are connected, the more healing can occur. We can be a wall and stop the healing or we can open the door and invite it in. We simply need to believe that we can be healed. The power of our soul/divine spirit brings limitless healing.

Points to Ponder

- Do you look at your life as a Gift? What else do you consider a gift in your life?
- If you had to identify the energy in your body, how would you describe it?
- Can you identify a spiritual guidance yet?

Chapter Two

Suffering is Highly Addictive and Totally Unnecessary

✿ ✿ ✿ ✿ ✿ ✿ ✿ ✿ ✿ ✿ ✿ ✿

When you live unconsciously, it is a melodrama filled with all of the upheaval you wished you did not come to know. Your presence is mandatory.

✿ ✿ ✿ ✿ ✿ ✿ ✿ ✿ ✿ ✿ ✿ ✿

As you read these books you'll continue to increase your knowledge and understanding of the depth of what we are discussing. You may feel a bit lost at times. Don't worry. It isn't just you. We all start from a place of unconsciousness and come to our place of awakening and healing slowly, step by step.

If we have lived lives in which we have suffered greatly then that is our set point and we bring suffering into our storyline. That suffering needs to be healed and learning how to heal the suffering is one of the lessons that we need to learn in this life. If we believe our storyline to be real and believe we should always expect suffering, then we project the suffering into our lives. This is the power of our mind and our ego. Believing makes it real, makes it happen on some level. If suffering is a set point then we become addicted to suffering. We subconsciously (and sometimes consciously) believe that is our life.

We have learned about schemas, (Jeffrey Young) which are like a blueprint of our self. If we believe A, B, and C about ourselves then we will fulfill the prophecy and A, B, and C will be confirmed. We will even develop specific patterns and coping skills for A, B, and C. We will choose things unconsciously through our Ego to confirm our life story and collect supporting evidence. If we believe we are going to get hurt in some way and live in fear of that happening, then we will call the hurt to us. Our projection and expectations of an event makes the possibility of an event more likely to occur. Our life is also preset to give us these opportunities for healing, to awaken us.

We have the power to manifest our thoughts and feelings by projecting them onto others and events. We can create problems out of nothing just to satisfy our addiction to suffering or victimization. Looking back, I felt that life was a struggle, that it was hard. I kept projecting this into my future, bringing or reacting to events as if they were difficult when it was unnecessary. This is how strong our minds and the power of belief really are. We keep recreating the same reality for our selves over and over and over again, physically, emotionally, and spiritually. The old energetic storyline and belief is strong and our ego loves to play that storyline out because ego lives in fear. Each time we play out the storyline, we entrench the belief even deeper into our subconscious. If you grew up with chaos your ego will constantly keep creating the same feelings you had as a child because that is what it knows. Due to the fact that the past is happening simultaneously with the present and future, you can see why the feelings feel so strong. Ego believes you are unsafe and wants to protect you from pain, but does so in a way that actually causes you more pain. Because of ego's projections and ways we choose to react to them, the end result is that we keep creating painful scenarios.

We are creating our own pain. We are the unconscious authors of our stories. This is how strongly and how insidiously we are programed to listen to our ego. It all needs to be changed. Our ego knows nothing about our precious gift of life. It only knows that it doesn't want to lose control. It doesn't want you or it to die.

We can only overcome our programing by becoming present and conscious and connected to our spirit/soul. This often requires that you believe the opposite of what you are feeling in a sense. If we are feeling pain, suffering and loneliness, when there is no true reason for it, we have to recognize that these are just familiar feelings that are really untrue. What lens are you looking at your life through? What are you doing that might be creating these feelings rather than looking at what is happening around you? I like to believe and project that my life is filled with dignity, grace, elegance and ease. You have to believe this more than you believe your original set point. We manifest what we truly believe. I can tell you that I see this working in my life everyday.

Believing what we aren't seeing can be a real struggle. You'll need every moment, every ounce of spiritual help that you can access to help you with this. This is how you learn to trust that you really are safe, loved, protected, worthy and powerful and that your life is graced with so much that you don't see. This is how you internalize the truth that you have divine powers within you and all around you, and that there is grace for every single cell in your body. This is where you get your reassurance that allows you to believe the best and not the worst about yourself, others, or your life.

Embrace the grace you were given even as you waffle back and forth between consciousness and unconsciousness, between old set points and new ones. Never give up hope. Keep practicing; keep working at it. I won't lie to you. It can be an extremely difficult and frustrating process. You'll feel that you are running a race inside of you to let go of the ego and the ego is holding on for dear life. The race will only be won when we let go of listening to our ego and stop giving it power over us, when we stop listening to everything it is projecting about us and others. Ego creates problems when there are no problems.

Keep moving forward no matter how many times you take steps backwards. Be loving to your self and understand that your ego is filled with all of the fears that you created by your programing, energetic transmission and responses to life experiences. It's amazing, but when you're finally freed from your ego you'll feel like a part of you has died, and it has in a sense. You may actually feel grief. But this is part of the rebirthing process and it takes time. You will emerge as a butterfly with new wings and a new story.

We can actually go though many periods of rebirth as we cut and prune away parts of us that no longer serve us. One by one we're removing beliefs established by the ego, programming, transmission and experiences. Over time, your old energetic/vibrational set points will keep losing their dominance and power over you. This can only happen by going inside and receiving help to understand who you are and gaining strength from all the divine support that is given and within you. Each rebirth is nurturing and empowering.

Points to Ponder

- What are the ways you feel like you have suffered in your life and feel that you are still suffering today?
- Are you living consciously or unconsciously?
- Can you tell the difference of when your ego is in charge

Chapter Three

Nourishing Your Self

❋ ❋ ❋ ❋ ❋ ❋ ❋ ❋ ❋ ❋ ❋ ❋

See the essence of who you are everywhere,
For everywhere is where you see yourself.

❋ ❋ ❋ ❋ ❋ ❋ ❋ ❋ ❋ ❋ ❋ ❋

If our set point is suffering, then we fill our lives with negative and a painful storyline. For many of us, our eating habits are merely symptomatic of our physical, psychological and spiritual pain. What type of foods do you need to eat? Do you eat things that aren't good for your body; things you are allergic to? Do you starve yourself, restrict food, or over-indulge and then feel shame and guilt and the need to purge, or stuff more food on top of the pain?

If suffering is your set point, you are only inflicting more pain and damage on your body, psyche, and spirit. Your ego is making your decisions and choices for you. It is playing a game with you and telling you that you are entitled to binge or eat or drink things that aren't good for you. Your ego tells you, you've worked hard, you deserve it, you'll be fine; tomorrow is another day. We listen and agree that our ego is right, but all we are doing is causing ourselves more suffering, shame and guilt. Or, do we withhold love from ourselves by starving ourselves of the nourishment we need.

We believe our life isn't perfect and we use food and drink, among other things, to undermine it even more. Our ego has an excuse for everything to help distract us from the inner pain and the accumulated negative energies within. Unfortunately, ego also distracts us from all of the gifts in our life.

Our behaviors with food and drink are just one way we malnourish ourselves physically, emotionally and spiritually. We live as though we are in a constant state of emergency. Everything has to be done now, right away, and then we launch our selves into our next distraction. While we bounce around in this distractive state of high anxiety, we are making other choices for ourselves that are not healthy.

Even exercise is done at a fast pace or excessively. We tell ourselves that we need to get our heart rate up. Imagine what your heart rate is all day while you live your life in a state of emergency or suffering. It affects every cell and organ in your body. We are so used to moving at an accelerated pace that we are burning ourselves out, all the while believing that this movement, this pace, is good for us because we are being productive. In Volume 2, I discussed how all of this stress and anxiety are releasing Adrenaline, Cortisol and other damaging chemicals into our body. We can actually become addicted to cycles of creating stressful incidents in our life in order to subconsciously stimulate the release of Adrenaline and Cortisol so that we can then experience their effects on our system. We become completely exhausted by living a life filled with an endless cycle of stressful events. We're exhausted, we don't sleep well or we sleep and do not feel well rested.

I borrowed this analogy from a friend. Think about a light bulb, and the electric energy that produces the light. Sometimes there's too much wattage for a light bulb causing it to burn intensely but then burning it out quickly or causing it to explode. Or, there might not be enough energy and the bulb's light is very dim, it's dull. We are doing both things to ourselves. Some people use drugs or other ways to artificially create excessive amounts of energy designed to make them feel good or powerful. Others use the same methods to deplete themselves of having any energy at all; they're essentially unconscious and trying to escape and avoid life. Some are doing both.

It is all another ego-lie that is reinforced by the programing of our society and culture. There is nothing nourishing about it. It is like we are living in a hamster cage, cycling on our wheel, and causing ourselves more pain and suffering. We are running away from our pain and suffering. What we fail to comprehend is that the faster we run away from our pain, the closer we bring it to us, it keeps coming up inside us..."Hey, I'm still here, look at me, I am not going away!" When we lack spiritual balance, we invite all kinds of other pain and problems into our lives as well.

I am not recommending that we stop all our fast-paced activities, but we need to find a balance. We can only find that balance on the inside, coming from a place of calm and peace. We have to find our core, our center, and then live from that place.

Your ego doesn't care about your health. Your ego is confused. In trying to protect you, it will give you heart attacks, strokes, disease, misery and suffering (all the

Adrenaline & Cortisol is contributing to many of the illnesses we have). It doesn't care that its choices are killing you. It thinks it is protecting you, that it knows what's best for you. It will indulge you in things that are not good for you. It will give you a false sense of entitlement all because it wants you to avoid confronting and dealing with your emotional pain and your shadow side.

Ego will stop you from doing nourishing things for yourself, since it believes you don't need those things. It will not let you be quiet and calm in a place where you can engage in your passions, seek your guidance, or go about things in a healthy manner. That is why we don't complete things we are working on. We get off task, go on and off diets and exercise programs. We can't stay focused when we're at the beck and call of all the erratic thoughts and mind chatter from the ego. One moment it is permissive and the next it is smacking your hands with a ruler!

It's time to unplug our selves from our ego. This means we have to practice being quiet, meditate, be still, so we can nourish ourselves with peace, calm and wisdom and stop the toxic flow of Adrenaline and Cortisol through our bodies.

When I first started to do this work, I recognized that I had been carrying anxiety and worry since I was five years old. I always had to be doing something or focused intensely on something to distract and hide those feelings from myself. That means I had been releasing toxic chemicals inside of me for years, my body was under stress. Eventually, it caught up with me and affected my thyroid and adrenal glands and I had a mini stroke about four years ago. I looked fine on the outside and was killing myself slowly on the inside.

Take out a piece of paper and think about your day, how you go about it and the thoughts behind the choices you made. What warp speed have you been moving at? If not physically maybe you are going at warp speed in your head! Do you really believe you have to move at that pace to get everything done? If you took your heart rate at any given part of the day would it show that your cardiovascular system is under stress? How about your blood pressure?

These are very important things for all of us to notice and observe. We need to raise our awareness. Sometimes, people feels so depressed and anxious that they become stuck, trapped and don't move. They sit on the couch watching TV all day or don't get out of bed. The suffering inside their heads is causing damage to every part of them. Our muscles start to atrophy and then it hurts when we try to do something. We all need to move, to live our daily lives, but we need to do so at a balanced pace.

Points to Ponder

- What is the role of suffering in your life? How long has it been there?
- Do you live your life in a state of emergency? All the time, sometimes?

- How do you numb yourself to the suffering or to the pace at which you're living? Is it with alcohol, drugs, sleep, people, food, exercise?
- Did you know that a healthy state is calmness, peace and contentment? Our energy should be centered in peace.

Chapter Four

Where Does the Role of Suffering Fit Into Our Soul?

*Do not make promises to
anyone else but yourself
to be who you truly are and
believe that it is enough.*

Our spirit/soul never suffers, but it does evolve watching us suffer. Our spirit/soul is never harmed, however it can become so buried deep within us that we don't know it exists. The spirit/soul understands both the spiritual world and the human world. It is always ready to help us, but if we are not in tune with it we don't hear it. Another name for our spirit or soul is intuition; it is all the same. Our intuition comes from our soul.

Our soul is beautiful. It knows what we need, what is best for us. The reason the soul has taken on a human experience is so that it can evolve in consciousness. Our storyline, our illusion provides a context within which the soul is able to evolve in wisdom and consciousness. You might imagine your soul as a child (inner child) that is growing up inside you experiencing your life, being a witness to your life, but it is never harmed and is always connected to God/Spirit and knows its divinity and the gift of life.

Remember, the soul doesn't get harmed by suffering, but can learn from witnessing the human suffering taking place. We grow through pain. It can make us stronger and wiser if we are able to process it, understand its origins and see it for what it really is. Unfortunately, many of us get stuck in our pain in a way that inhibits our growth.

I know that this too is difficult to absorb. Why would our soul need to take on human form if it is pure spirit and a divine being of goodness? It just does. I don't have that answer. Maybe we simply forgot that we are divine. Being in human form on this earth is the soul's university for learning and evolving. As the heavens are infinite, so is knowledge and wisdom. Our souls keep evolving; the evolution never stops. That is why we incarnate again and again.

What does it mean to incarnate? Incarnation is when a spirit takes on human form. Please remember, we are dreaming this, (See volume 1 and 2 for more information). I know this is complex.

We…God/Spirit/Universe are all one, all the same. There is a divine being of goodness (God/Spirit) within each one of us. Again, the job of the spirit/soul is to incarnate as necessary to gain the knowledge needed to evolve consciousness.

Since the ego is part of our human nature, it provides limitless opportunities for our soul to experience and witness pain and suffering...countless opportunities for our soul (and for us) to grow and evolve. One might easily look on this as being a negative if you believe that life is something other than an illusion. Life, as we most often perceive it is not reality; it is your pre-birth storyline and the continued storyline made up in your ego / human mind.

Much of the pain and suffering comes from the belief that we have or will experience pain. It is like reading a fascinating book of fiction or watching a compelling movie and believing that what you read or saw is real. The story in the book or the plot line in the movie isn't real. It's just a product of our ego's imagination and projection based on our wounds, programing and transmitted energy.

It takes time to allow this wisdom to integrate into you. As we evolve we are ascending to another floor on the elevator of consciousness. It needs to sink in. You should meditate on your questions to find truth. You should discuss them with your spiritual guidance. Allow the information to percolate within you. After a while you will see the truth as the veil of unconsciousness continues to lift.

It can shake you up a bit if you start looking at your life as a farce and not know what to do or feel about it. Integrating and understanding that you still have a role to play in society is your purpose and it is very important. You just go about that role in a new, more balanced and creative way. You can now create a conscious storyline and shape your dream with God. You can let go and just be. You can express your love and your gifts to yourself and others in a much more nurturing way. You can have a loving heart for humanity with the understanding that others are still asleep and lack awareness. You can't shake or force anyone awake. They will come to it, or not, on their own, in their own time, just like you did.

Keep focusing on your self and pray for others that God/Spirit will keep working in their hearts and guide them to consciousness. Pray for the greater good of the planet. Keep digging inside your self to continue to evolve. You will experience loneliness if you are alone in your evolution on earth. It is good to find others that are on the same path as you who can help you with your continued evolution. While your human-side may feel alone, your spirit never does because it is always plugged-in to God/ Spirit and knows that it is never alone. Your spirit does not experience loneliness.

Your job is to take over, transcend the ego, align with your spirit/soul (the highest part of you) and stay connected to truth. We need to discipline ourselves and not listen to our ego anymore so we can mature and allow love and light to flow from our soul. This task may be difficult and it takes enormous effortful control every minute of the day until you have become more aligned with the highest part of you. We need to lovingly re-parent the wounded child parts within us and discipline ourselves to let go of the ego and its belief systems, the delusion. Navigating this can be very difficult. How do you operate in society as you are learning all of this? You have to keep focusing on yourself all of the time.

* The inner child is the unharmed young child within us that still remembers being one with God and all creation, it is part of our soul.

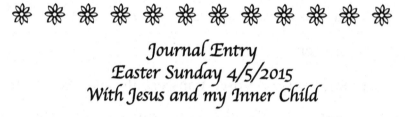

Journal Entry
Easter Sunday 4/5/2015
With Jesus and my Inner Child

My Inner Child talking to me: I love you. You are a child of God. You are precious, divine and worthy. It is God's joy to see you happy and in love with your life. But what is life? Most of us do not know what that is. It is all the love in your heart that gets scattered and given away or locked away so no one, not even you, can feel it. We were made to feel that love and share it with others. We forget that is why God created us. It's very simply, just love; yet it can be one of the hardest thing to accomplish. Some hearts are fresh and have not been tainted, therefore these people can feel and give to others but most have stopped this flow of loving energy even to themselves. We want to help people fall in love with themselves, with God and others. To do this we must learn how to evolve our heart, our soul. We do this by helping others and helping our self. We must see through the illusions of life that love is the ultimate answer. We must rescue our heart in order to move forward. God rescues our hearts but only if we allow him. He calls on us daily to see and hear. We have learned not to listen or see all the magical miracles he has created around us. We are asleep and unconscious, we wake up and get a glimmer of the Truth, we go back to sleep, yet we yearn for the love and happiness that is right in our very souls. It is amazing and it is sad. We resist help, we stop the flow; the energy is always there within. We feel helpless, as if we are blind. It is so powerful and moving to watch. **Me:** Why do we do this? **My Inner Child:** We do it because we feel grief and loss from the illusion of being separated from God's love. But the truth is that we are never separated from God. We never were and never will be. We feel those things for no true reason. We are children looking to everyone else and everything else to fill our love. We forget who we are, where we came from, and focus on things that don't matter and cannot take the pain and fear away, yet we continue to do it. It is a blessing and a misery. Being in denial, an illusion can help us feel that we are not in pain, but it is untrue. Ultimately, it brings more misery to our hearts…the loneliness of not knowing God's love. God gave us our will and that will is exceedingly strong. It is so strong in fact that keeps us locked in these trances. Our trance can only be unlocked through God's love, yet we keep escaping back to old ways and old habits that do not work for us, Debbie. It is imperfection at its finest. This is what being human is about. We are lost in a world out of touch with why we are here. **Me:** What can we do? **My Inner Child:** We can let go and let God take over. It sounds easy but it isn't. All the negative forces of life keep dragging us down…wanting things, thinking it will make us happy. True happiness comes from within. Even if we have all our desires met, what good is it if we do not feel happy? We are clear about what does not make us happy yet we continue to do things that continue this pain. Humans are amazing creatures of habit. **Me:** What is it that we are writing, Jesus? What is my Inner Child trying to tell me? **Jesus:** It is a soulprint. **Me:** What is that? **Jesus:** It is the story that our souls carry around that contain the misbeliefs about our selves… the misbeliefs that we need to change and overcome. **Me:** Where did this soulprint come from? **Jesus:** It is hierarchy, it is inherited through generations of suffering and strong wills. When God gave us free will it was to be used for good and love. The suffering caused the will to be discharged in ways unthinkable. **Me:** God must have known this. **Jesus:** Yes, but He has given everyone a loving heart and believes if followed it will prevail. **Me:** Today I heard the story of Cane and Able. Why did Cane have suffering and want to kill Able? Where did the suffering come from? **Jesus:** He was filled with resentment when God rejected his sacrifice; he did not know God in his heart. **Me:** So this has been an affliction since the beginning of man? **Jesus:** Yes, there has been much suffering in this world since the beginning of time. Fear, darkness, lack of safety, they all were and still are problems. These have been with man since the beginning and are like a fierce energy living inside of him. **Me:** This story you are telling me, is it just for me or for others? **Jesus:** It is how I want you to understand our world. You will need this in order to understand people better. Most act out of fear, just like you, but it does not have to affect you if you understand it has nothing to do with you. If you understand this, it will positively affect the way you see yourself and others. It needs to change. Your heart needs to absorb this knowledge so you can grow more. **Me:** I understand. We are all fearful of many things, some more than others but we all experience fear. I am not to judge it. **Jesus:** Yes, not to judge it within yourself or others. **Me:** So when I am confused and don't understand how I am feeling or what to do, is it okay? **Jesus:** Yes, it is okay and there's nothing wrong with it. That is why you come to God to help you with your pain, confusion and to help you with the answers. No one else can do this for you. This is why you bring us to your client therapy sessions. You are there to comfort them and to reflect that what they are feeling is okay. God will heal them if they allow; you cannot heal them. If this is not the time for their healing, then you just provide comfort. **Me:** What else is there for me to know to focus on? What will make me happy to do, what fills my soul with passion? **Jesus:** Good question. Singing, dancing, telling stories, having fun, loving others, being in the water, art, travel and new experiences. You like movement and you are stuck in keeping still. **Me:** How do I mix my soul's purpose of being loving and a comfort to others with my soul's passion? **Jesus:** Try dancing in synchronicity to the story of God's love so that you can feel the love and passion through movement. Let yourself be swept away by the grace and movement and the feelings of love that fulfills your soul. It is beautiful. Me: How do I learn this story or dance? **Jesus:** You already know the story and you feel it in every part of you, but you stop yourself, you don't let go, you are reserved and fearful of judgment. When you let go it will come. **Me:** How do I let go? **Jesus:** Practice, go in your room, close the door, put music on and dance. **Me:** Is there a teacher or someone to help me with letting go with my body, mind & spirit. **Jesus:** It is already happening through massage. **Me:** What kind of music? **Jesus:** You will know it when you hear it.

Jesus showed me visually what kind of dancing he was talking about. I would describe this as a modern type of dance. Very slow dance movements to relaxing music. It is wonderful and I love doing it.

Points to Ponder

- What thoughts or feelings come to your mind when I talk about incarnation? What are your beliefs?

- Have you ever heard your soul talk to you? If you have, what did you hear?

- Did you know you can have conversations with your soul any time of the day? It knows everything about you and what is best for you.

- It is your job to fall in love with your soul and it is easier than you could ever imagine since it is pure love and light.

Chapter Five

Becoming Whole

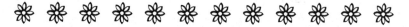

*Holding onto life, people and things is
just an illusion that will always end.
The only thing we should
hold onto is being love.*

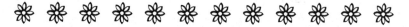

Owning your truth of who you are is like learning to walk all over again. We stumble, trip and fall all over ourselves and everyone else. It isn't a graceful process although it is filled with more grace than you can ever imagine.

Your ego worries "What will people think about me if I speak my truth? How will I handle it? Can I handle it? People will think I'm crazy." Ego's questions bring out all of our fears and insecurities. Not everyone wants to hear what you are learning or doing, and that's okay.

This is a process of trial and error, and your ego is always getting in the way. We are still projecting our fears and insecurities onto everyone because our process of integrating and understanding all the wisdom we are learning is not yet completely in sync and hasn't taken root. We waffle in our own belief system, swaying from consciousness to unconsciousness. We take baby steps each day, putting our toes into the waters of consciousness. Some days we fall face first into the pool and drown; other days it comes more easily. We have to take it one day at a time.

Your spiritual guidance is always there to pick you up, brush you off, love and reassure you that what you are going through is all quite normal. We are always looking on the outside for someone to validate us, to tell us we're not crazy, we're not alone, to take responsibility for our feelings. As you go through this process you eventually come to understand that it is nice to receive the external assurances and for a while they carry you, but it does not carry the same weight as the support you get from your spiritual guidance.

Receiving support from our spiritual guidance is like drinking from a well of divine nourishment. We need to fill our tanks each day. This is an eternal, never-ending supply of divine nourishment that will give you the power to continue your work and the confidence to live your new life.

Again, we can access our guidance through breathing, prayer, meditation, stillness and creating. Think of your guidance as a beautiful white or golden light, a divine light. You inhale that light with a deep breath and exhale out anything that is not serving you. Keep breathing in this light that is surrounding you. Use your imagination to see it. It is yours to take at any given moment of the day. Go to it often; it is your divine right. Fill your self up with it. It doesn't matter how many breaths you take. Breath until you are replenished, until your tank is full of peace and love.

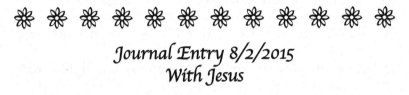

Journal Entry 8/2/2015
With Jesus

Me: What is wrong with me this week? I feel so emotionally unstable, up and down, minute-to-minute. This is something I experience off and on and it can last a day or a week! It is almost like being hormonal monthly but I am way past that. Please help me understand. I need more light on this. What do you think it is? I know that I am going through a lot of changes internally and externally. **Jesus:** Do you not see all the changes coming and happening in your life? **Me:** I do. I just think I should be handling it better, easier, smoother. **Jesus:** Why? **Me:** I guess in the past I would notice I was not doing well from feeling it through stress and being uptight. **Jesus:** That is because you were not feeling your feelings. You kept them wrapped-up in your body. **Me:** So are you saying if I don't acknowledge my feelings, if I do keep it in my body (which I have done my whole life) then when my feelings do come out it is causing this up and down emotional rollercoaster? **Jesus:** Yes. Your feelings are right under the surface. So they are triggered and then they feel erratic and overwhelming. **Me:** How do I get better at feeling my feelings so this does not happen anymore? It is exhausting! **Jesus:** Believe in yourself. **Me:** How does that change my ability to handle my feelings as they come up? I thought because I had been working with all of my wounded selves, healing and loving them I was dealing with my feelings. **Jesus:** You don't realize how much more there is to heal. You need to continue spending time with all of your wounded selves more often, continuing to love and heal them with me. **Me:** How do I do this? Please show me, I am feeling overwhelmed just thinking about doing this. **Jesus:** See, you believe you cannot manage your feelings! **Me:** You are right! I can manage them and have had good success healing myself so far. I am just not used to feeling my feelings on a day-to-day basis. I am still suppressing **Jesus:** Every time you shut down to you, you shut down to everyone else. You need to keep digesting this information, understand it and when you start to feel anything, explore it. You keep asking us to tell you what is wrong but if you take time and go inside yourself you will figure it out.

This is an example of working with my six-month old self. My arm was broken somehow at birth. It turned into a bone disease called Osteomyelitis located in my left elbow. I was in a lot of pain for months until the doctors finally diagnosed the problem. Physical pain started at birth for me. What I am sharing now is similar to what Margaret Paul would call her six-step Inner Bonding technique. I am using visual imagery and am holding my six-month old self. Now, of course, she can't speak but I am hearing and knowing every word she says. I hear her cry out inside me.

Me: My six-month old self had so much physical pain. She cries out to me to help us. I need to take care of myself better so I do not have pain, like my skin, my ears (psoriasis). She is such a brave little girl, went through so much pain, cried all the time. All I could do is cry. I couldn't stop the physical pain. **My baby self:** I need you not to cause me any more physical pain by holding our feelings in our body. I can't take it any more, all I want to do is cry. I wanted everyone to know how much I hurt and make it stop! It hurt so bad, touch, everything hurt me, getting dressed, movement, make it stop, please. I don't want to hurt anymore. Please take care of my skin it hurts so bad and you keep ignoring it; WHY? My scalp, head, you don't put medicine on there either! All you care about is your legs, face and arms the places that people see, but I hurt other places. MAKE IT STOP, PLEASE. I want you to stop pushing down all our feelings; that makes me hurt too. And that pillow, why can't you ever find something to rest our head on that doesn't hurt! You are never sitting right and that hurts too. Please stop hurting me. **Me:** (I am speaking to Jesus now). I am comforting my baby self, rocking her. If I believe I can't stop or comfort my own pain how do I help people find comfort and compassion for their own pain? Thank God that He stopped the pain from that bone disease. I need to be grateful and take better care of myself to be pain free. I can't keep holding my feelings in my body. I need to address them.

Points to Ponder

- Have you been noticing the ups and downs in this process?
- How are you doing with taking responsibility for your feelings?
- How often to you meditate to talk with your guidance about what you are feeling?

Chapter Six

How to Hold On to Your Light

❀ ❀ ❀ ❀ ❀ ❀ ❀ ❀ ❀ ❀ ❀ ❀

There is a light within me that illuminates
It is God's love and fills every
empty void within
It sweeps me into His awesomeness
of love & peace

❀ ❀ ❀ ❀ ❀ ❀ ❀ ❀ ❀ ❀ ❀ ❀

I often imagine myself at the beach, the sun shining brightly, a beautiful blue sky. I allow the sunlight to encase me with its warmth and I breathe in the light until I am refreshed. This is one of many visualizations I use in my meditations.

CREATING A LIFE WORTH LIVING

Our spirit/soul needs light all the time. Darkness doesn't refuel us. Even at night or on cloudy days, it is good to use your imagination to enjoy some light, even if you can't actually go outside and get a few minutes of sun. We always need to have light in our lives.

Light opens us up with brilliant peaceful energy and awareness. It guides us down paths we need to travel. We need to drink-in the light and call it in to us as often as we can. Light expands us; darkness contracts us.

As I was doing this work, God taught me that I need to stay in the light. I would practice using my imagination to go to the beach each day and I would bring God, Jesus, and my higher self to sit with me so that I could drink in the sunlight and open to receive their wisdom. At bedtime, all my vulnerabilities would emerge, I had trouble sleeping. I would be scared with all of the uncomfortable energy that needed to be healed circulating within me, (although, I did not understand what it was at the time). The incessant mental chatter would keep me awake. This also was a cry for help from my wounded children that I did not recognize at the time.

I found myself visualizing nighttime at the beach curled up in God's lap with Jesus and my higher self. They brought me love and safety. I created a beautiful fire to create heat for us since the nighttime was cool.

I used this guided imagery for quite a long time. Nighttime was very scary for me. I had wounded children inside me who were still fearful from past experiences that I had not healed. I used my imagery to bring me to a place where I could find safety and peace at night. Eventually, God told me that I needed to create light at bedtime, in the dark of the night. I needed to vision the beach as it is during daytime so I could have sunlight. The fire I had created wasn't enough light.

At the time, I didn't understand why God gave me those instructions, but I do now. Our ego lives in darkness. Within that darkness there is no truth or clarity. The wounded parts of me were used to living in this darkness and they needed a lot of light to heal and gain wisdom. The light is our life force in many different ways. It is hard to conceptualize all that the light brings us. We, and everything else, need light to survive. The light of the sun gives life to almost everything living on the planet.

God/Spirit created the sun, the moon, day and night. The daily cycle gives us time to rest at night to recover from and to replenish all of the energy we use during the day. Sleep time is supposed to nourish us. We rest so that we can go about our work the next day.

For many of us, nighttime turns into a difficult part of the day, especially if bad things happened to us at night or in the dark at some earlier point in our current life, or past lives. Many of us have trouble sleeping. We can't calm our minds. We are hyper-vigilant. We have nightmares that bring negative, fearful, uncomfortable energy flows through our body and make it difficult to rest and sleep. Or, maybe we rehash everything about the day, the past, and then worry about the future.

During the day it can be easier to shut off all that haunts us because we are distracted with the everyday things of life. At night there are fewer distractions, so we're left with our storyline, our worries, fears, anxieties, our projections and everything else we have not dealt with yesterday, today and tomorrow.

These days most of us spend a lot of time on computers and using other technology that exudes a different kind of light, and it interferes with our sleep clock. I've found that for me, it's best if I don't use my computer at least two hours before going to bed. Restful sleep is vital. It affects so much of our mind and body's functions. We don't appreciate how much energy we expend during the day. If you aren't consistently sleeping well, this should be a red flag that something is going on within you that needs to be examined and resolved. You need to shine more light on the situation.

Many people simply start taking sleep aids or using alcohol to fall asleep, however, this doesn't solve the underlying problem. When younger I used pot to try to help me sleep when I couldn't sleep. It just made me unconscious and pass out. It didn't fix the problem. You have to go inside to find out why you aren't sleeping well. If you anesthetize yourself with drugs or alcohol, you take away your ability to look inside you and identify and heal the underlying problem.

Everything you deal with on a daily basis is meant to help you wake up. Everything we experience and everyone we encounter throughout our day is there for a reason, as are our feelings. Start taking closer notice of your daily thoughts or encounters. Ask yourself, why is this happening, and then pursue the line of thinking in an effort to understand what you are meant to learn from the encounter. There is so much to be discovered within; you need to start digging.

Start with the questions: "Why do I feel_____? Why do I think_____? Why do I behave_____? Fill in the blanks and make a list.

After you have your list you can then ask yourself "Why don't I correct this?" What's the true answer? Sometimes we're afraid to ask these kinds of probing questions because we don't really want to know the answer. It's OK to be afraid, but be brave and courageous. No one else has to know your answers, and it will help you get to the source of your truth.

As you work your way through the process, you will come to understand your storyline and how things came to be. But as you go up the elevator to another level of consciousness, you'll begin to understand that you are not just dealing with your present existence, your current reality. Your spirit/soul has experienced any number of prior incarnations.

If we are incarnating, then we may have lived many lives trying to learn lessons that have become part of our present storyline and part of our present energy.

As energy is transmitted through families generationally, then each of us have been touched by generations upon generations of other people, some good, some not so good. Some of that energy resonates with us more than others. Your Spiritual Guidance knows and understands all of this about you.

About a year ago I went to a Salt Cave with a good friend of mine and didn't really know what to expect since it was my first time. You go into a room the size of a large bedroom that is made of Himalayan Salt. It is set up for you to relax and meditate as you recline on a lounge chair for about 45 minutes or an hour. It is very dark in the room. There were no other people in the room with us, but when the door was shut and I was incased in the darkness some wild fear energy came over my whole body that affected my breathing and peace. I did not understand why I was feeling this way.

The fear seemed to come out of nowhere. I felt like I had to get out, like I was trapped and in danger, my ego had taken over. I heard Jesus' say to me, you are okay, you are safe calm yourself and to take deep breaths, that I was not in danger and that it was simply an old fear resurfacing. I did what I was told, calmed down and was able to defuse the energy by deep breathing and enjoyed the rest of the time in the Salt room.

What I noticed during this spiritual journey is that there are times when an energy that had previously been repressed can take over in a split second. You start to pay more attention to the energy running through you as you become more conscious and it is always leading you to something that needs to be healed within.

Points to Ponder

- What are your thoughts about light and darkness? What are the parts of you that live in the darkness, our shadow side?
- Can you identify energy as it is coursing through your body?

- Now that you know it is important to work on that energy to heal and dissipate it, how will you make time for it?

- Do you have trouble sleeping?

- Did you fill in the blanks from the question in the mid section of this chapter?

Chapter Seven

Transmuting and Transforming

If I told you that your journey
was just a dream
What would you create?

Transmuting – to change from one
form to another; to take the raw
material of an experience and transform
it into stories; to change the form,
appearance, or nature of something.

The role of transmuting is important; it's like an angel getting its wings in a sense. Many of us have watched the classic Christmas movie 'It's a Wonderful Life' starring

Jimmy Stewart. In the movie, an angel by the name of 'Clarence' is sent to help the character 'George' through a difficult period in his life. Clarence's job is to clear away George's negative thoughts and feelings so that he can see his true purpose in life, that he indeed was a blessing to others, and recognize that he is surrounded by love and blessings. When George finally succeeds in his task, Clarence earns his angel wings; he evolves to another level.

What do you suppose Clarence's lesson was? He too was a blessing and didn't realize it. As he learned how to keep following God's word, he saw grace for himself and George.

This is what is happening with all of us. Our transmutation starts when we ask for help to transform all of our negative programing, patterns, thinking, feelings, behaviors, stories, vibrational inheritance and energy. In the movie, as George received help from Clarence, he was also helping Clarence in his effort to evolve.

The process works the same way for us. When we humble our selves and reach out for and receive help, we are helping others spiritually. We may not see how we're helping a spirit, but we are. It's fascinating, isn't it? God/Spirit is indeed amazing.

For example, my spiritual guidance has been Jesus. As I learn my lessons, Jesus evolves as well. There is a connection to my lesson learning as a student. As I heal, forgive, and reach higher levels of consciousness I am also moving energy through me. This allows growth for His spirit to evolve through higher consciousness and energy. My transforming is creating more light for others.

It is fascinating to see that our growth helps the past as well as the future and present. My father and other family members that have passed on have thanked me for what I am doing because it elevated them in some way that I do not truly understand. There is a collective consciousness whether you are alive or not and that it is universal, not just of this earth.

If you are scratching your head, it's okay; so did I. I couldn't understand that Jesus would need to elevate anymore. As I mentioned before, all spirits evolve because knowledge is infinite. It is okay that you are looking up into the elevator shaft of consciousness right now wondering how to get up to the next floor. I certainly did. Sometimes I feel like I get stuck between elevator floors of higher consciousness. I find that I may be able to understand a difficult concept to a limited degree, but my understanding isn't complete, it isn't clear yet.

Jesus explained to me how this helps Spirit but because I cannot put it into a form that I (my ego) can understand, I haven't integrated it; I just believe that it is truth because it came from Him.

Everything may not make sense right now, but it will. Keep meditating on what is being discussed here and a clearer understanding will come in time.

There are many who can help you in removing/transmuting and transforming all that is no longer serving you. Make a list of family, friends, whomever, who has passed on, as well as your guidance. Include them in your prayers with God. As you do this, you are also clearing out old energy and patterns that keep past loved ones stuck. You are also clearing out old family energy that has been transmitted to your children and grandchildren, etc. You will be asking for a blessing and giving one at the same time.

Pray that all of the negative patterns of our planet be transmuted as well. It is a step towards peace and it's a beautiful thing that we have the power to do this. 'Heal me, heal the planet.' Imagine the impact we could have if we all added this to our prayers each day. You are asking to heal all of the false beliefs of your ego's programing, the storylines, and for everyone to awaken to consciousness and peace. I can't imagine a more gracious way to start one's day...by spreading love. Barbara De Angelis has a beautiful community prayer for the planet daily.

Our spiritual guides work with us to help us and while doing so, they advance in their own evolution. We'll have many guides throughout the course of our journey. If we learn the lesson(s) that one guide has to teach us, other guides will appear. Think of it as being in a school where you have a different teacher for different subjects. It is the same in the spiritual world; as we master a lesson, another teacher comes. I have had many lessons from several spirit guides/angels, God/goddess, even including deceased family members who love me and help with the healing during my journey.

We never lose our guides; they're always with us. As we learn our various lessons, some guides come to the forefront as needed and others move into the background. You can always call on them at any time. You don't have to worry about any of this. Your new teacher will arrive at the perfect time when you are ready in your spiritual world and our earthly world.

It's uncommon for us to learn a lesson completely without having to revisit it time and time again. We all get triggered back to old behaviors or thoughts and feelings where the need to remember and re-learn old lessons will resurface again. We never truly master everything in our lifetime, so it's normal to fall back into negative patterns even if we've been doing well avoiding them. That's why we always need to ask for transmutation during our prayers and meditations.

Points to Ponder

- What feelings or thoughts arise in you when I speak about transmuting and transforming?
- Are you willing to do this work so that your family members that passed, the ones in your present, and future generations are cleared out of the vibrational inheritance that was passed on to you and what you have passed on?

- Can you look at this as something you are doing for the greater good of the universe...out of love?
- Are you recognizing how much power you really have?

Chapter Eight

You are Blessed

*You are the artist of your life
What will the canvas look like
when you are done?*

*Divine Providence – is the governance
of God by which He, with wisdom and
love, cares for and directs all things
in the universe (GotQuestions.org)*

We are all so blessed and don't understand how blessed we really are. All of God's grace surrounds us daily but we don't see it. There is *Divine Providence* in every moment of our day. We are distracted by everything...our thoughts, the incessant mind-chatter, and the noise of the outside world. We miss so many opportunities to see the miracles that surround us every day. As you practice being present/conscious you will get glimpses of this. You'll begin to see the magic and synchronicity in the natural world and recognize that everyone around you is truly an angel supporting you.

When you see this you feel profound joy and love. You begin to realize that your perception of how you've been seeing and experiencing your world is not reality. It's like some one just turned on the light switch and now you're seeing truth. Little by little, the veil continues to lift.

That truth has always been there but because we are so stuck in our head and storyline/programing, we can't see the forest through the trees. Even though we may get glimpses of the truth, it's very difficult to consistently stay at that level of consciousness. It takes practice. We go up and we go down. We take so much for granted that truth slips away from us, and it may be quite a while before we're able to see it again.

We need to make a conscious effort each day to remember that we want to stay in truth and allow our self to feel joy and happiness. Our ego is constantly trying to strip our joy from us. Wake up everyday and remind your self how beautiful and magical earth truly is and how very lucky you are to witness this, to be a part of it; to be alive, to stop taking it for granted.

One way to work on this is to stop seeing your self as broken, as a victim of circumstance, and by the way, no one else is broken either. We are all playing a role in your storyline and you in theirs. Everything is as it is supposed to be. As a dear friend of mine Mari-Etta Stoner, says, "Everything is working perfectly". If you focus on being a victim and suffering, that's all you'll see around you; and that's what you'll bring to you. Make the decision that you don't want to live that type of life anymore; change your storyline.

We can change our storyline anytime by changing our perception, by changing everything from negative to a positive perspective. Look for the good and not the bad. Look for what is right in your day and not what went wrong with it. Nothing has to change, only you. Now of course this doesn't mean that you won't have to deal with life. Events still happen in our life.

Keep shifting your perspective; it's very simple. It's a skill you need to develop on a daily basis. See and acknowledge all of the grace and blessings in your day. Once you start doing this, you'll get hooked because it makes you feel great, and you'll want more. It's a great way to bring peace and serenity into your life.

What will you do with this knowledge? Can you accept it or will you continue down the same path that is damaging to your self and others? What is standing in your way of accepting the blessings? Are you thinking that you aren't worthy to receive them? I did.

I went through this process myself. I felt I needed proof. The proof was right in front of my face every day but I couldn't see it; I denied it. I had to have constant reassurance that what I was learning and witnessing was truth…that I was worthy of this truth. My ego didn't want to accept the truth and kept pulling me back into my storyline that made me think I could blame others for the way I felt or that something was wrong with me when there wasn't. Ego would not let go of the illusion, would not accept that my 'reality' was really just my story, projected outwardly.

Failing to let go of your story and the justification and reassurance that your story gives you is what keeps getting in the way of your seeing all of the miracles, blessings and grace that surround you. We keep looking to others to learn our truth when it is staring us right in the face. We are blinded by our story and the ego's delusion. Imagine how freeing it is to know that whatever suffering, victimization, or lack you may think you are experiencing is not really happening, you are projecting it. It's part of your storyline, unless of course you're in a violent situation. If that's the case, you then need to remove yourself from it.

All of the negative programing that comes from what you think is happening to you or who you think you are or what you deserve can all fade away. We can finally let go of all of the wounds and battle scars we've accumulated and been carrying around with us all these years. CHANGE YOUR STORY! CLOSE THE CHAPTER! START A NEW BEAUTIFUL STORY/LIFE! LIVE THE DREAM IN YOUR HEART!

Points to Ponder

- Can you find evidence of grace throughout your days?
- How would you describe the grace that you see? Can you hold onto it each day and expect to see more?
- What is the storyline you are cultivating?

*Please see http://www.everythingisworkingperfectly.com

Chapter Nine

Truth or Dare

Inner peace is all that one needs to attain.
The rest will be a breeze.

Let's discuss why it's easier to hold onto the illusion/delusion: 1. We think it gives us justification for what we do, think or feel; we believe it: 2. We don't want to give up control: 3. We don't want to look at our life as being untrue: 4. We don't want to let go of anything: 5. We can't see the bigger picture.

If our lives are an illusion, it means that everything is different than what we think it is, and as a result, we don't know how to be or who we are. This can feel pretty scary when you are dismantling yourself and realize that you are not sure who you are then. As we keep growing and feel more comfortable accepting truths about our selves through our spiritual guidance, the process of letting go of the illusion starts to happen naturally. We realize that others don't define us and therefore we don't define others. We are no longer responsible for others and they're not responsible for us. We no longer see things as obligations because we are now living from our heart.

If you've come to see this as true and have integrated it into your wisdom, I then dare you to go back to living your life the way you were before you awakened. Would you, or could you do it? Do you want to go back to sleep? Most of us would say 'No.'

If you are one of the one's who say 'No', you should then be motivated and inspired to keep digging for more truth and divine wisdom. This is what helps separate us from the delusion. Do you want the illusion of battle scars to still define you, or would you rather see your divinity and create a life built on love, truth, purpose, and passion? All you have to do is accept that you hold the key to unlock your new life.

This is a huge quest so I do not want to minimize it or say how easy it is, but no one else has your key. Your spiritual guidance has been keeping the key safe for you all along, and has the map to show you how you get there.

So, will you dare to dig deep, discipline yourself, and let go of your ego? Or will you let your fears stop you? Your guidance will help you take the leap of faith and trust that will allow you to come into who you truly are, and receive all of the gifts that await you.

You won't take that leap without a safety net or parachute, your guidance is always there to guide you. Little by little, with each passing day, you move closer to all of your dreams. I dare you to dream big and, no matter what you come up with, it won't compare to the greatness that is already planned for you.

One thing I've learned is that I didn't have to be totally proficient in developing all of my skills, acquiring wisdom, or separating myself from my ego in order to make the transformation happen. It just starts to happen as you do the work. I'm still me, but with a different perspective of my self and of life. My heart opened and grew as I allowed it to, as I kept feeling safe and reassured by my spiritual guidance and Barbara.

One of the most significant parts of your life journey is to grow your heart as big as possible. I'm not perfect as a human being, far from it; but as a divine being of goodness, I am. I still make errors, my ego hijacks me at times and I go back to being unconscious. I am not always in my highest, although, that is what I strive for. Nevertheless, I am still growing spiritually, and the more I come into alignment with God, my highest, my truth and purpose, the more my life keeps changing for the better.

You don't have to evolve in your consciousness to a certain level before you start seeing positive changes in your life. It can happen quickly. My progress accelerated when I decided to make this work my job, my primary job,

(And yes, I have a full time job). I focused and practiced daily on what my intentions were for the day. I wrote in my journal and meditated and prayed daily until those practices became an integral part of my daily routine. I didn't pass judgment on my self as I began to recognize my negative programing. I simply made note of it. I allowed others who understood this process from different perspectives to help me. That was crucial in reassuring me that I wasn't going crazy, that others had experienced the same things during their spiritual awakenings. I had never let anyone in before. It was a huge leap of faith that has paid off in my evolution.

All of this allowed me to keep deepening the trust and faith in continuing this work. I sought wisdom deep within me, not just from the outside world. Trust your guidance. No one else knows what's best for you. All your decisions need to be made with your guidance's help.

I'm now completing the second year of my personal spiritual journey. I'm a better person now than before I started. I'm more full of love, joy, and creativity that ever before. My journey is to maintain and integrate what I've learned. My goal is to continue to grow my heart and consciousness. It's a humbling experience. I am so grateful for the unconditional love, dignity, honor, and grace from Spirit that is always there to help me along my path.

Points to Ponder

- What thoughts or feelings arise when you think about life as an illusion? What is your ego saying?

- How do you feel about dismantling yourself so that you no longer believe the delusion of who you are? Does that bring up fears? What are they?

- Have you been spending time with your spiritual guidance talking about this? If not, why?

- Would you dare to go back to your previous state of unconsciousness, although I know it is one dare that you will not want to take.

Chapter Ten

We Are All Cosmically Connected

Policies Do Not Apply To The Spiritual Realm

Yes, we are all cosmically connected by the same energy. The source of that energy, God/Spirit, connects all of us. Spiritually, we share the same parent in a sense. This energy is cosmic love and light, and it carries an enormous amount of power. What we are trying to do is reconnect to that power so that we can collectively have a profound affect on the energy of the planet. Earth is also energy. It is comprised of the same energy that we are.

Seeing life on earth as a collective entity rather than as a separate collection of individuals is part of your growth and lessons on a human plane. If you recognize that you are part of humanity collectively then you can fulfill your purpose by using your gifts to help others feel connected and not alone.

I know this sounds very 'New Age-ish', but it's time to see that you have power. That power is the love and light inside you and you need to stop withholding and judging it. It's the power that lives in our heart. You can't be afraid to share it with yourself and others, although, this is what most of us do.

We're meant to share our eternal love and light. That is our purpose here on earth. As you awaken to your gifts you will see powers within you. You can enhance those abilities through many of what you might call 'New Age' skills, plus many skills from more traditional teachings and customs as well. Or you can let your spiritual guidance show you. Those abilities are already inside of your spirit/

soul. They are part of who you really are, your true nature, a sacred divine being of goodness.

These abilities make us powerful teachers, healers, leaders, and coaches. The list does not stop there. Anything you can offer in creativity through your heart affects others profoundly. Until you come to understand your life's purpose, your heart is your most powerful tool and can be offered to others.

Others need what you have to offer as a gift for them to grow and awaken. That is why I have 'birthed' these books; and believe me, it was a birthing process. Waking to our gifts can be laborious, but it's worth all of the labor pains because it is a blessing. Each word comes from a source of love and light to help you on your own journey. It is the same light that lit the path for me; it is Jesus' light.

Some people would call this 'Christ Consciousness.' It is an understanding of life and our own divinity through Jesus' teachings (not religion) and using His principles as we make our way along our own individual path. If you can see that we are all one, then you understand that how you treat others is the way you want to be treated, i.e. with love, compassion, dignity, and honor. We need to see that we are not the only one's who have suffered, and that, collectively, we have all suffered and still are suffering because we mistakenly believe we are disconnected from God/Spirit, the source of Love. Feeling compassion for your own and others' suffering is key. We need to move from just seeing our individuality to understanding that collectively, I am you, and you are me. If we all come to this understanding that we are part of a collective whole, we can heal our selves and the planet, and elevate the universe.

Points to Ponder

- What thoughts or feelings arise when I talk about collective consciousness? What does your ego say?
- Are you willing to explore how you affect the greater good and visa versa?

- What is your understanding of the power that each one of us has? Did you know that the only true power comes from your heart through love?

- Are you able to show yourself compassion and regard? How about to others?

- What is your talent or purpose? Have you discussed this with your guidance?

Chapter Eleven

Branching Out to Bigger Space

*You are beautiful and loved more
than you can ever imagine,
See what happens when you
really take that in.*

If we can move from looking at just our selves, our family and friends, our own little world, to the whole of this world, we can then come into seeing that whatever our gifts, they are urgently needed. Whether your gifts are meant for a single person, or for all of humanity, they are needed. We need to overcome our ego and its fears to be able to utilize these gifts. Remember, our gifts are not for us alone, they are for everyone. I had to overcome my ego's fear of writing these books, and branching out. It was not easy, but I had to keep pressing through it. That doesn't mean that I do not come face to face with my fears at times either.

You might say this is all idealistic thinking, however, it is the truth of what we are here to do. If you think your purpose is otherwise, or that you have no purpose, then your ego is in control.

We are all the same, no one better than another regardless of skill level. It might be that someone has a very unique gift or they are more aware in their consciousness, but that doesn't make them better than you or more valued than you.

Our programing has taught us all to measure our selves against each other. We have to be the best at something, a winner. We have to have more money than the next person, or receive a trophy or a medal or some other recognition that gives us some sort of elite status. While competing in life can be interesting, it really reduces us to seeking the approval and acclamation of others. It leaves us searching for something we have done or accomplished that makes us feel good about our self or better than others rather than coming from a place of purpose. Wouldn't it be better to approach life from our heart, with some wonderful talent to share, or by overcoming a fear or a disadvantage?

If we haven't accomplished what others have, then we see ourselves as losers, not good enough. Even if we are accomplished, many of us still somehow don't feel quite good enough. That's how I spent much of my life, measuring my self-worth by what I accomplished on the outside, not on the inside.

The interesting thing is that the more we do accomplish, the more we just keep raising the bar higher and higher for ourselves. Even though we have achievements to our credit, peace, contentment and happiness still elude us. This is because we see our selves as not being good enough in the first place. We don't see that as spiritual beings we are already perfect and don't need to prove our worth to our selves or to others, we just need to be who we truly are.

We need to expand our vision of how we see the world and each other. We aren't in competition with each other. We're here to help each other heal from our suffering and pride and replace it with love and expansion and humility.

We all suffer. When we expand our vision to see that it is not just me who suffers, we start to feel connected. Because we have pride, most of us wear a mask that hides our suffering and therefore we become judgmental of others and ourselves. We only see our own suffering. This is all part of the immaturity of the ego and what needs to be disciplined.

By realizing that we're here to help each other overcome suffering and share love and light, we change the vibration of the planet to a more positive state and increase the collective awareness and consciousness. Just by you changing, your perspective will shift other's perspectives and create a domino effect toward positive change.

This has already begun. There are numerous people, groups and organizations trying to raise consciousness and awareness in various locations all across the planet. Regardless of whether their message resonates with you or not, they are all trying to raise awareness and expand consciousness.

How would you like to see the world? How can you expand your vision to look at life in a more collective way? How do you want to envision and live your life so that your children and generations to come can have a better life on earth? We all play a role in this. We all need to move from a 'me' to a 'we' perspective in order to expand. This is how we bring hope to the world.

Our ego is selfish; it lives in smallness, in a little microcosm of life in which it feels safe and comfortable. We need to break out of the smallness. There are so many others who can benefit from your love and light. Start journaling about this. Start having conversations about it with others. It doesn't matter if they disagree. They may not be awake yet, and that's okay. The more you start talking to others you'll find like-minded people who will inspire you and give you energy to shift your consciousness even further. Stick your little toe into the water and feel around. It's time for you to branch out and expand your self, allow your spiritual guidance to help you.

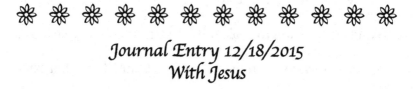

Journal Entry 12/18/2015
With Jesus

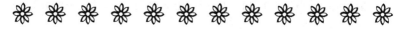

Jesus: This process is not perfect and you need to look at each accomplishment of seeing and not what you have achieved. This is more of your victimization patterns. **Me:** There is so much, so, so much. **Jesus:** Yes, it is what happens when we leave our ego in charge. As you see, it is not just you. **Me:** It makes me want to cry. It is so sad and frustrating. **Jesus:** Yes it is. How do we focus on the blessings that you are seeing and not on what you have not accomplished? **Me:** I guess I need to be more grateful for all the miracles in my life. I let go of gratitude in a split second as I go unconscious again. **Jesus:** Yes, that is why staying present is so important and we are thrilled with your progress. You expect too much. You do not understand the magnitude of what you are doing, how long it takes, or that it is an amazing undertaking. **Me:** This appears to be a theme in my life, not respecting my process. I need to sit and digest and be. How do you recommend I do this? **Jesus:** Just what you are doing now. We have been doing this quickly because of your classwork (I was taking a college class at the time), and not taking the time necessary. Why do you think you should accomplish these abilities all ready when people have worked all their lives on their spiritual journey? Are you better than anyone else? **Me:** No. What then am I trying to prove by putting pressure on myself or the pace of how this goes? I have always had to do things fast, from being a youngster had to move and think fast, never knew when something bad was going to happen; it was a strategy, a coping mechanism to survive fear. I had to be the first one done with a test in school when I was younger as if it gave me something special because I finished quicker than anyone else. This pace is irrational. It makes me physically ill. The work I am doing today is not for attention or recognition I am doing this for self-growth. I keep thinking I want to be better, healthier emotionally, which makes me feel that there is something wrong with who I am now, hence the victimization cycle continues. It is entitlement, as If I am special and "should" be able to do this quicker. It shows no respect for the process or honor of myself. I even come to you Jesus the same way at times when I have to make a decision about something. 'Here's the problem Jesus; what do you think?'…as if everything is a life or death decision.. I'm not trusting my own intuition when I know it is very strong. There is still a lack of respect for myself. **Jesus:** I think you are seeing very well. This issue with time and pace is all about not having to deal with your feelings and keep safe. This is not your life anymore. You need to focus on staying still, just being, talking less. You are no longer in danger and most of the time you are in gratitude and happy; there is nothing to run away from. We are here to catch you, we sit with you, walk with you everywhere. **Me:** I know that and I love all of you. I feel very safe. **Jesus:** We will work on these patterns to transmute them one day at a time. Remember, dignity, grace, elegance and ease. Slow down. Stay in the light. You do not have to worry about a thing. Stay with us on this island in your heart and mind so we can lead you. Just like you are doing now. This is where you are grounded.

❀ ❀ ❀ ❀ ❀ ❀ ❀ ❀ ❀ ❀ ❀ ❀

Points to Ponder

- Is there a fear of moving your thinking and creativity out of your smallness, the box we keep ourselves in? What are the fears? How does that stop you from feeling fulfilled and happy with your life?

- Where have you been putting your energy in trying to prove yourself or get ahead? Or, have you not invested in yourself?

Chapter Twelve

What a World We Live In

❋ ❋ ❋ ❋ ❋ ❋ ❋ ❋ ❋ ❋ ❋ ❋

There is nothing more powerful than Peace.

❋ ❋ ❋ ❋ ❋ ❋ ❋ ❋ ❋ ❋ ❋ ❋

I know much of what you've read so far may not make sense to you. That's primarily because we were never taught this at home or in school. No one knew; your parents didn't, your teachers didn't. It just wasn't on the agenda; it wasn't a part of our programing.

Even when truth is spoken, most of us reject it. We reject things that we don't or won't understand; it's a part of our human nature. So how do we integrate something we don't understand?

We can integrate by writing about it and talking to others who are on similar journeys. We can research questions and issues, and then take them back to our spiritual guidance to ask for the truth. Integration takes time, so be gentle with your self. Sometimes we just need to let the questions, issues, and answers percolate within us.

The process also shakes up your reality and belief systems, but they need to be dismantled, reexamined and reorganized anyway since they contain very limited truths. Everyone has her/his own belief system, or if they don't trust or understand what they think and feel, they simply borrow a belief system from someone else. This is what I have done most of my life since I did not trust myself. This all takes time.

If everyone were to ask inside them selves for the truth about this world, we would all basically hear the same thing since it is coming from the same collective source. As humans, we are stubborn; it's our ego...stubborn as a mule. We live in a world where we judge good or bad, right or wrong, black or white because we look at things on the surface within society's framework and through our own pain, guilt and shame. These frameworks were developed in an effort to maintain some semblance of order, power and stability; that's all they are.

If you know your life is just your storyline, a dream, and that each person is just acting out her/his storyline as a character in a book, how would that change the way you witness behavior in this world? If you understood that everyone is reacting to their own perceived suffering and their behavior is an attempt to take away or hide their pain, do you think you might look at yourself and others differently? Would you, could you, develop compassion for everyone's ignorance of the fact that they are asleep and unconscious? Could you develop compassion for your own unconsciousness?

Would it help you to transcend judgment of yourself and others if you knew that each person is playing a role just for you, and you for them? Would it help if you understood that your job is to look deep into your soul so that you can awaken and heal from your story of suffering? Imagine what this could mean collectively if each of us could transition to compassion, love, honor, and forgiveness. Grace is not just something you say, or receive; it is something you give.

Wouldn't we all love to get a second chance, a do-over? Well, here it is; the process of awakening is a second chance for your self and others to be who you were meant to be and not who you thought you had to be.

This is cosmic grace. You get a second chance to become the love and light you were supposed to be. Will you grab that chance or will you not trust it, just like you haven't trusted other things in your life? Will you let go of your illusionary suffering, the delusion, your story, or will you cling to it? Your choices will make a difference in how you experience the rest of your life.

How does clinging to the illusion benefit your self and others? Do you prefer freedom for your self and the rest of the world? Your act of letting go will influence others to seek their freedom from suffering.

This doesn't mean that bad things won't still occur in your life. It does mean that the impact that those events have on you can be greatly minimized. When we let go of our old pain and suffering, we empower our family and friends to do the same in their own time. Isn't that the most wonderful gift you could give them? All you have to do is want to heal your pain and the rest happens from there.

Would you rather look at this world as a mess that you are caught up in, or would you like to see it as a miraculous place that you are positively contributing to? You have that much power, and it needs to by used thoughtfully by understanding the secrets of life and awakening to your purpose. We are all vessels of love and light, and we need to reconnect with that truth for it is the only truth about us. It is all we have and are. It will never change. It is our divine gift given to us for all eternity.

❀ ❀ ❀ ❀ ❀ ❀ ❀ ❀ ❀ ❀ ❀ ❀

Journal Entry 2/21/2016
A visual interaction With Jesus

❀ ❀ ❀ ❀ ❀ ❀ ❀ ❀ ❀ ❀ ❀ ❀

Jesus: Come with me. **Me:** Where are we going? **Jesus:** You will see, take my hand. (We go into outer space and are looking down on the planet. My biological father attends as well). God's Spirit is everywhere throughout the universe and that Spirit does not die or fade. The universe is inhabited by spirits which all have their own purpose, just like yours. Some are older and some younger. Most of these Spirits have been born and incarnated over and over and over again on earth trying to learn the soul's lessons of love and light and to become one with God, which transcends everything else. Some achieve this and some don't but some incarnate to learn very quickly and for others it can be hundreds of thousands of years. Some of the spirits in the universe therefore are not as enlightened as others and still carry negativity or are less harmonious. Spirit is energy and what happens is like finds like so there are clusters of spirit in different parts of the universe. They await until they can incarnate again. Until then, sometimes they may travel in a way, to see what else exists in the universe. This is why you are so important. Your light shines so brightly, it illuminates different paths of travel and it alerts a spirit to something that is harmonious or not; this is very important. **Me:** I really do not understand all of this. It is hard to believe that some places in the universe "are neighborhoods you don't want to go into". **Jesus:** I know that does not make sense with God's power but it happens and sometimes spirits from these "neighborhoods" infect earth. **Me:** So the same thing that happens on earth happens in the universe? **Jesus:** Yes, in some way, but luckily there are much less of that kind of spirit. **Me:** Do you have names for different types of spirits? **Jesus:** Yes. **Me:** What are they? **Jesus:** That's not important now. We will talk about that at another time. You will have another guide/teacher for that. (At this point, I am glad the conversation ended about that since I had no desire to know any more weird stuff). **Jesus:** I wanted you to see why we need to keep your energy pure and why finishing these books are important. I want you to make these books your job, but I want you to still feel happy about it: it is a blessing. **Me:** I have no problem with that. They are a blessing. **Jesus:** The earth basically became a cesspool of disease, war and negativity. It was not what it was created for and it needs to ascend to become filled with light and love. There are thousands or millions like you that are trying to uplift the world each in their own way and it is of the upmost importance to do this now.

(He called me a 'lightworker.' I was not even sure what that really meant, in fact I am not sure I understand much about souls yet).

Points to Ponder

- What is your belief system or programing telling you upon reading this?

- How do you see the world?

- Are you willing to take the second chance you are getting to create the dream of your life?

Chapter Thirteen

Ode to Jesus

❀ ❀ ❀ ❀ ❀ ❀ ❀ ❀ ❀ ❀ ❀ ❀

You have come into my life and brought so much love and beauty. Words escape me, for I have never witnessed this before. It is a blessing more than I could have ever known. Imagine, all I had to do was say 'Hello', and it changed my life forever.

❀ ❀ ❀ ❀ ❀ ❀ ❀ ❀ ❀ ❀ ❀ ❀

Why would someone want her/his life changed so profoundly? Is your life filled with unconditional love, grace, beauty and abundance? If not, ask yourself, why? You might not have known it's yours for the taking; I certainly didn't, but it is.

I had been listening to Joel Osteen over the past few years and heard him speak about this, however, until I opened up to receiving my spiritual guidance, I didn't understand it. God's/Spirit's love and abundance is there for everyone who wants it. There is no magic to it, and not just one way to get it or experience it. It's all there waiting for you. It is a tragedy to me that we have such little awareness about this.

There is nothing special about me; I'm just like you. I just had a passion to heal myself and kept digging deep down inside me. I also had a dream to expand from seeing individual clients in my counseling practice to finding a way of helping many people at the same time. I had prayed to God for 15 years that I be given something to help many people at the same time and hopefully sustain me while doing so. Thirty years ago I started praying for healing and direction. I never imagined it would be through this spiritual door. Although I prayed all the time for help, I resisted walking through doors that were outside of my comfort zone. I was stuck in my smallness and allowed my ego to guide me unconsciously, unknowingly. I had bought into the illusion and delusion. I never really allowed anyone to help me because deep down I never trusted anyone.

The first time I heard God speak to me was in November 2014. I was home sick for a week with laryngitis. I stayed in bed resting for the week however I was working very hard using an at- home program from Margaret Paul to increase my vibration with meditation. I also was working on Derek Rydall's 'Soul Purpose Blueprint', another at-home course. His course uses a lot of visual guided imagery as well.

I had been praying and meditating to God non-stop that week that I am ready please, please show me my purpose in life. All of a sudden I heard "Are you ready to listen?" I said 'Yes', and then I laughed because I finally understood that I had not been receiving, I never listened to anyone including myself. My ears had been closed for so long, since childhood. God has a great sense of humor. He told me to write down everything I hear. I heard the voice of my Inner Child (about 3 years old) and she dictated to me a beautiful children's story about God. I have not published this yet, but will someday. I am so happy that I finally decided to listen. It has changed my life profoundly. I needed to get out of my own way.

I'd like to spare you from your suffering by sharing all of the wisdom I have learned from Jesus, God, my other spiritual guides, Margaret and Barbara. There is no time like the present, and it's free. It doesn't cost a thing to meditate and open your self up to the love and freedom that waits within you. You can find examples of free guided-meditations on YouTube. Keep trying different ones until you find something that works for you. There are also free yoga lessons on YouTube as well. Your ego might be blowing this off, but don't let it. All you are doing is just trying something new that can bring wonderful changes to your life.

If you are reading this book, than you were led here because you are ready and are looking for a purpose and meaning for your life. You are tired of the suffering from being disconnected from love, spiritual love.

Everything you need is within you. Stop running away from your self. Your spiritual guidance is waiting for you patiently to unearth the secrets about your true self and the world. Stop resisting the temptation to do something more loving for your self than you can imagine. Don't make any more excuses. It's your time, and you are being called upon to finally show up and accept your divinity and gifts. Don't give your ego power over your choices. It's time to put your foot down and follow through for once without giving up. It's time to complete your journey.

I'm telling you this because I have experienced seeking, praying, paying, and reading, and never following through. My ego would hijack me and I would stop or I felt some emotional pain and would run the other way. I used excuse after excuse for why I didn't have time for my self. The reason was that I didn't feel worthy and wouldn't give time to my self, didn't know how and was comfortable living in denial, comfortably numb. I looked high and low but always looked outside of me and never inside. I never believed I could handle my emotions or pain, so I avoided going inside. When I did look inside I thought I healed myself but I did not, I only scraped the surface. What I learned is that its all a lie from our ego, none of it is true. We can handle our pain and joy. You will find the same thing because we are all the same; I am you and you are me. We are divine beings of light and goodness.

Our egos are the same as well, full of false programing. Something to keep in mind again is that your children, your spouse, partner, family, friends and coworkers are all doing the same thing. They are all being led by their egos. At times you may get a glimpse of their souls, and as you do this work you can see the goodness in everyone and see the best in them. With some, it will be more often than others. Have compassion and regard for your self and others by doing this work and learn how to put your spiritual guidance first because that is putting yourself first in becoming prepared for success in every area of your life.

Points to Ponder

- Are you ready for a profound change in your life?
- Are you willing to do the healing work?
- What have you tried to spiritually connect?
- What is blocking you; ask your spiritual guidance to show you

Chapter Fourteen

Blessings

❋ ❋ ❋ ❋ ❋ ❋ ❋ ❋ ❋ ❋ ❋ ❋

"I pray that God/Spirit bestow onto (name) the blessings that have been bestowed onto me. Heal me and heal (name)." This is a prayer Jesus gave me to bless others. This prayer is for you. Please take it and use it for others. Every time you use the prayer, you are blessing others and your self.

❋ ❋ ❋ ❋ ❋ ❋ ❋ ❋ ❋ ❋ ❋ ❋

I silently use this prayer all day long blessing people with whom I come in contact. I bless my family, the planet, people I pass on the street. It feels good to bless everyone and every thing. It's worth taking the time to do. You never know the impact you might have on someone's life. This is what this work is all about, sharing your love and light, and inspiring others. It is speaking love and hope to those who are suffering. By doing this, you build compassion and humility within you and begin to expand the smallness in you that keeps you thinking only of your self.

We all fear what to say or do, but if your kindness is coming from your heart and not from your ego, that's all that matters. When you try this at first it doesn't matter that it might be coming from your ego. Keep trying and you will see your heart open. When you are trying to speak with your spiritual guidance at first and are not sure what you are doing, it feels like you are making up conversations in your head. That's normal and it doesn't matter whether you are or aren't. Eventually, you will know that you are not making it up. It's all trial and error. There is no perfection to this; there is no deadline. What matters, is that you keep expanding your self with love towards your self and others.

Don't judge yourself as you are practicing having grace for yourself and others. Unfortunately, we were never taught how to do this. We never witnessed it enough to learn it. Eventually, all the rough edges will smooth out. That is what your spiritual guidance is for. You see so much grace given to you and role modeled daily that you just start to do it yourself.

Your spiritual guidance is constantly helping deal with your ego if you allow it to. Your ego can be extremely mean, but your spiritual guidance, will handle your ego with grace and then help you with disciplining and love. You will be so much happier when you begin to see how your grace starts to be translated on the outside of you. Just the action of blessing people each day changes you and changes them. Even if you are having a struggle with someone, bless her/him and then let go of it. You will feel lighter and then you are on your way to healing. If you hold on to grudges, anger and suffering you are causing damage to your self physically, emotionally, and spiritually. The only one who is suffering is you, and you are causing it. Your energy is then toxic too so others get effected by it.

As you start down this journey of healing and letting go, many of your ailments will be healed as well. We need to let go of emotional pain in order to heal our physical and spiritual pain. Yes, I believe God/Spirit can heal everything within and without. It just takes time practicing letting go and turning within to your spiritual guidance and moving away from your ego.

In your imagination, open your heart with breathing, see yourself in a beautiful relaxing scene, peaceful and reach your hand up over your head and invite whatever spirit is there to guide you to grab your hand. When you feel something, pull your hand down to see who is there. Try this several times until it works within your imagination, and it will work if you have an open heart to it. While you are still using your imagination open your imaginary eyes and see who you allowed in to help you. Don't question who or what it is. Just know that they are there to love you. Look into the light or into their eyes and reach out to them. All you have to do is say: 'Hello. Thank you for being here, what do you have to share with me today" and let the conversations begin.

Points to Ponder

- What is your belief about prayer? Do you pray? How often?
- What thoughts or feelings arise when I talk about opening your heart? Is there fear? What is it about?
- What else do you do to help you think about others and not just your self? The world?
- What do you think would happen if you actually saw or heard your spiritual guidance?

From my heart to yours – I love you

The next part of your spiritual

journey will be found in Volume 4

Tuning into Your Intuition

*See you there, I'll be waiting
for you with more love ....*

Printed in the United States
By Bookmasters

Printed in the United States
By Bookmasters